Emotional Intelligence 2.0

A Practical Guide To Understanding Your Mind Secrets, Sharpening Your Mental Skills To Perform Better At Work And Improve Your Social Life

By Daniel Cloud

CONTENTS

INTRODUCTION

Learning processes are incredibly complex because they are the result of multiple causes which are articulated in a single product. However, these causes are fundamental of two orders: cognitive and emotional. Despite this, the prevailing educational model, in general, tends to ignore or minimize the psychological aspects and to the extent the student rises within it, these are less and less taken into account.

However, because of the educational revolution generated from the emergence of constructivism and the impact of the theory of multiple intelligences, a new debate has opened in pedagogy that includes the role of emotions as one of the fundamental aspects to be considered in the integral education of the student.

As is proper in the social sciences, defining mental constructs to work with is a difficult task, and emotions do not escape this dilemma. No one doubts that all human beings experience their existence. Although we cannot always control their effects, hence the importance of considering their emotional education as such an essential aspect in the formation of the individual, just as much as the academic education, for constituting a whole person who is so intimately linked to each other, that it would be unthinkable to consider the possibility of developing any of these aspects separately.

And since the educational act is only possible thanks to the presence of the two main participants: learners, and educators, it should be considered as the second influencing the emotions and feelings of the first, within a specific cultural context, which is ultimately the place where you define what we assume as being emotions and feelings.

CHAPTER 1
EMOTIONAL INTELLIGENCE EXPLAINED

Emotional Intelligence is one of the key concepts to understanding the direction psychology has taken in recent decades.

From a model mainly concerned with mental disorders on the one hand and reasoning abilities on the other, we have moved on to another one in which emotions are considered to be intrinsic to our behavior and non-pathological mental activity. Consequently, feelings are something that must be studied to understand how we are.

Thus, Emotional Intelligence is a construct that helps us understand how we can adaptively and intelligently influence both our emotions and our interpretation of the emotional states of others. This aspect of the human psychological dimension has a fundamental role both in the way we socialize and in the adaption strategies to the environment in which we live.

We have always heard that Intellectual Quotient (IQ) is a trustworthy indicator to know if a person will be successful in life. This quotient is based on the intelligence score, which is said to establish a strong relationship with overall instructional performance and professional achievement. This concept is not in itself incorrect, but it offers us a biased and incomplete picture of reality.

Researchers and corporations began to detect a few decades ago that the skills and abilities necessary to succeed in life included others that went beyond the use of logic and rationality, and these capabilities were not evaluable by any test of intelligence. It is necessary to take into account a broader conception of what basic cognitive skills are, and what we understand to be intelligence.

Proof of this is that we began to gain some theories of intelligence by trying to understand it from different perspectives, such as the theory of multiple intelligences of Howard Gardner's theory of Raymond Cattell (and others) explaining the variations among fluid and crystallized intelligence, or the Emotional Intelligence popularized by way of Daniel Goleman.

In our everyday lives, we can quickly realize that there are many occasions when our feelings have a decisive influence on our actions, even if we do not know it. Many of our decisions are influenced to a greater or lesser degree by our emotions.

It needs, faced with this truth, to be stated that there are humans with an area in their emotional facet much more evolved than others. And it is curious about the low correlation between classical intelligence (more linked to logical and analytical performance) and Emotional Intelligence.

Here we could exemplify this idea by mentioning the stereotype of a "nerd" student; an intelligent machine capable of memorizing data and reaching the best logical solutions, but with an empty emotional and sentimental life.

On the other hand, we can find people whose intellectual abilities are minimal, but instead have a successful experience when it comes to their emotional sphere, and even their professional aspect.

This pair of examples taken to the extreme is unusual, but serves to realize that it is necessary to pay more attention to these kinds of emotional skills, which can mark our life and happiness as much or more than our ability to score high on a test of general intelligence. For that, it is crucial to deepen the look into Emotional Intelligence.

ELEMENTS OF EMOTIONAL INTELLIGENCE

The great theorist of Emotional Intelligence, the American psychologist Daniel Goleman, points out the main components that make up the Emotional Intelligence as the following:

1. Emotional self-awareness

It refers to the knowledge of our feelings and emotions and how they influence us. It is essential to recognize how our mood affects our behavior, what our capabilities are, and what our weaknesses are. Many people are surprised at how little they know themselves.

For example, this aspect can help us not to make decisions when we are in an unbalanced psychological state. Whether we are too happy and excited, or if we are sad and melancholy, the choices we make will be mediated by the lack of rationality. Therefore, it is best to wait a few hours, or days, until we have a relaxed and serene mental state, with which it will be easier to assess the situation and make much more rational decisions.

2. Self-control (or self-regulation)

The emotional self allows us to reflect and master our feelings or emotions, and not to get carried away by them blindly. It consists of knowing how to detect psychological dynamics, knowing which ones are transient and which are lasting, as well as being aware of what aspects of an emotion we can take advantage of and how we can relate to the environment to subtract power from another that harms us more than what benefits us.

To give an example, it is not uncommon to get angry with our partner, but if we were slaves of the emotion of the moment we would be continuously acting irresponsibly or impulsively, and then we would regret it. In a certain sense, a good part of the regulation of emotions consists of knowing how to manage our focus of attention, so that it does not turn against us and sabotage us.

3. Self-motivation

Focusing feelings on objectives and goals allows us to hold motivation and focus on goals in place of limitations. In this factor, a certain degree of optimism and initiative is essential, so we have to value being proactive and performing with dedication and in a high-quality way in the face of unforeseen events.

Thanks to the ability to motivate ourselves to reach the goals we rationally know benefit us, we can leave behind those obstacles that are only based on habit or unjustified fear of what may happen.

4. Empathy

Interpersonal relationships are based on the correct interpretation of the signals others express unconsciously, and often emit non-verbally. The detection of these emotions of others and their feelings that can be represented by signs that are not strictly linguistic (a gesture, a physiological reaction, a tic) can help us to establish closer and more permanent links with the people with whom we relate.

Also, recognizing the emotions and feelings of others is the first step to understand and identify with the people who express them. Empathic people are the ones that typically have higher skills and capabilities related to IE.

5. Social skills

A good relationship with others is an essential source for our happiness and even, in many cases, for excellent job performance. And this helps us to know how to treat and communicate with those people who we are close to, as well as with people who we aren't close to; one of the keys of Emotional Intelligence.

Thus, thanks to Emotional Intelligence, we go beyond thinking about how others make us feel, and we take into account that any interaction between human beings takes place in a specific context. Perhaps if someone has made a derogatory comment about us it is because he feels envious, or because he needs to base his social influence on this type of behavior. In short, Emotional Intelligence helps us to think about the causes that have triggered others to behave in a way that makes us feel in a certain way, instead of starting thinking about how we believe and from there deciding how we will react to what that others say or do.

Today many corporations invest large sums of money in training their employees in Emotional Intelligence. The reason for this wager is that companies have realized that one of the keys to commercial success and the sale of their products lies in the degree to which their workers can recognize and control their emotions, as well as the emotions of their customers.

It is almost unthinkable to conceive a salesperson who lacks skills in dealing with customers, an entrepreneur with no motivation for the management of his company or a negotiator who does not know how to control his impulses and emotions. All of the technical information based on the exceptional relationship among instructional studies and enjoyment will not be any guarantee for those human beings, due to the fact subsequently they'll destroy any economic operations they undertake due to having an inadequate knowledge of their emotions.

Is There Empirical Evidence To Support It?

The concept of Emotional Intelligence has empirical evidence of two types. On the one hand, it has detected the parts of the brain that intervene in its appearance and not so much in the other types of mental processes. On the other hand, by using standardized tests for their measurement and analyzing the data obtained, it has been seen that Emotional Intelligence has its factorial structure so it correlates positively with the general IQ scores, but statistically, it does not behave the same as what or who you are.

In other words, the psychological construct of Emotional Intelligence is based both on the observation of the functioning of the brain and on information obtained through psychometrics.

Of course, the same problems when defining general intelligence remain when explaining what Emotional Intelligence is. It is neither a part of the brain nor a concrete way of processing information, but establishes its existence by observing how to act in certain conditions and in what way that leads us to obtain advantages or disadvantages in a situation. The nature of Emotional Intelligence remains mostly a mystery.

Emotionally intelligent people understand four crucial things:

1. **You can read the emotions of others.** That's tough, especially when dealing with people who are not very emotion-oriented. It is easy to say that someone is sad when he cries, but how can you tell someone is heartbroken when he tries to hide it? Emotionally intelligent people can and with practice.

.

2. **Emotionally creative people are also able to understand and regulate their own emotions.** This means they are in contact with what they are feeling. Regulating these emotions is crucial - that is, you can wait until you get frustrated after the meeting because you know the consequences, when you show it at the very moment you first feel it. It also means keeping it together long enough to be there for a sibling when a parent is diagnosed with cancer, even if you feel the same amount of anxiety and sadness.

3. **Emotionally intelligent people understand that their thoughts** generate their emotions and that facilitating and controlling their thinking can lessen the power of their feelings. Moods and feelings can also enhance certain types of thinking: knowing, for example, that you can

handle conflicts better when you're calm and make decisions when you're not upset.

4. **Finally**, emotionally intelligent people understand the connection between their actions and the emotional responses of others. For example, they know that breaking a promise causes others to feel hurt.

Building emotional intelligence is a difficult task, but it's a great way to improve how you deal with others. One way to develop emotional intelligence is to watch your thoughts. Watch how your ideas connect with your emotions throughout the day. Thoughts release chemicals in the brain that fuel the way we think about things.

Once we notice the connection, we can work to diminish the negative emotions we experience by not giving power to the thought that creates negative emotions and by focusing on raising the views associated with positive emotions in the mind connection stand.

The issues of stress in the workplace are a real problem both for the well-being of employees and for the efficiency of the organization.

The existence of stress experienced by one or more collaborators is a sign of a problem that is often broader than the individual's ability to regulate his or her emotional states. We sometimes tend to shift the responsibility of stress to everyone else. We can then propose some sort of personal development tools to fight against this stress.

Even if each of us has a personal responsibility for his own emotional states and the way he regulates them, this should not mask the effects of the organization on the human being and the psychic constraints that may result.

It is therefore essential to fight against stress at work to be able to propose actions at each person's stress level and to also think about the organizational dimension and in particular its relational aspects.

Emotional intelligence is a tool particularly relevant for building relational contexts that fight against stress at work.

What are the determinants of work stress?

According to the National Research and Safety Institute for the Prevention of Accidents at Work and Occupational Diseases:

Stress occurs when there is an imbalance between a person's perception of the constraints imposed by their environment and the understanding they have of their resources to cope with it. Although the process of assessing limitations and resources is psychological, the effects of stress are not only psychological. They also affect physical health, well-being, and productivity.

Stress is a process that emerges in the individual when his resources to confront a given situation seem obsolete. It is the situation of inadequacy, which is at the origin of this experience, and it is thus highly subjective. These effects on the individual are, on the other hand, concrete and potentially harmful, whether related to acute or chronic stress.

On the individual level, we do not all have the same abilities to regulate our emotional states. This depends on how we are built as an individual and touches on several systems related to psychic functioning:

- Attachment strategies (behaviors and relational modes) that aim to regulate our states of distress by approaching a reassuring figure to find a security base. (attachment system)
- Mental models that serve us to make sense of the information produced around us, especially regarding the potentially threatening dimension of a situation. (threat system)
- The ability to perceive the sensory aspects of an emotional state, then to relate them to an emotion related to a given context. (Self-awareness about mental processes)
- The ability not to identify with a moving experience to be able to respond outside of automatic behaviors.

On the organizational level, all settings do not produce the same effects in terms of stress. The aspect I will stop at is how the organization builds readability and accessibility of available resources for each. The question of relational dynamics at work in the organization is central to it.

Organizational relational resources are primarily are the way everyone can rekey on each other in a stressful situation.

When our resources are exceeded, we become dependent upon each other to find a solution that can regulate our state. For us to allow ourselves to activate this dependence, it must be an acceptable choice in terms of measuring the consequences: can I let myself show my vulnerability? What will others think of my inability to resolve this situation? Will they have a negative perception of me?

In such a context, the social constraint of the gaze of the other and the judgment of the other take a central place in our decisions. The contrary hypotheses that can be formulated complicates and amplifies the stressful situation.

The culture of the organization plays a fundamental role in how everyone confronts this social constraint. It defines what is acceptable and what is not. A culture focused on relational benevolence promotes the expression of its difficulties and allows it to mobilize relational resources without fearing the consequences. A performance-oriented culture alone can make it difficult to verbalize one's disability, forcing the individual to fend for themselves in a situation that is beyond them.

The emotional intelligence of leaders and managers plays a role in the construction of culture and points of relational emphasis. Thus, the example we give is central to the development of representations within the organization.

What are the effects of stress at work?

The physical effects of stress are numerous and alter many physiological processes. The deterioration of a person's well-being is directly linked to it, in particular in connection with the loss of quality of sleep, the increase of cardiovascular and autoimmune diseases, or even the highest risk of infection.

The psychological effects are also present, particularly disorganizing relational processes. Indeed, the state of stress-related emotional hyper activation has a direct impact on how individuals make assumptions about their interactions.

The alteration of mental processes is responsible for it. These ongoing processes in the individual are used to perceive their mental states, those of others, and to conclude the most appropriate interactions.

The hypotheses formulated then naturally focuses on negative aspects, which represent a higher risk. This prism interprets each interaction.

This results in a significant loss of relational efficiency. Creativity is profoundly altered since it implies a risk-taking linked to novelty.

In addition to being yourself in this state, the effects of emotional contagion tend to hyper activate those around us, leading to even more significant disorganization of relationships.

How can emotional intelligence provide answers to these states? We must first define it further.

Several models of this concept, born in 1990, exist today. They overlap with the idea that emotional intelligence lies at the junction between emotions and cognitions: the way we think about our feelings and those of others.

It is a concept whose scientific foundations are still under discussion but which has the advantage of highlighting essential aspects of the psychic functioning of the individual, particularly in the professional setting.

It comprises four distinct aspects, which are then divided into competencies:

- Self-awareness.
- Self-management.
- The social conscience.
- Relationship management.

There are two poles: consciousness and management applied to oneself and someone else. Within its poles, emotional intelligence makes it possible to make sensitive contents accessible to thought (cognition), and to make informed decisions about these contents.

The self-awareness comes in a core competence that is someone's emotional self-awareness. The other domains are built on this pillar. It refers to the individual's ability to perceive their moving experiences and how they affect their functioning. It comes as much in the complexity with which we can label our emotions as in our ability to communicate about our emotions with authenticity.

The self-management covers the emotional management, the ability to adapt the face of uncertainty, a tour achievement orientation, and personal growth, the trend of having a positive attitude regardless of the situation.

The social consciousness is composed of empathy, especially in its decision-dimension into explaining someone else's perspective, and organizational consciousness, i.e., understanding the complex relational entanglements within a group.

Finally, relationship management includes the influence of the coach/mentor, conflict management, the team, and the inspiration capacity to others. This is the most critical dimension to support relational efficiency, but it is only possible if the other aspects are sufficiently developed.

Emotional intelligence develops throughout life, and it is possible to potentiate this development for personal growth. This conception is connected to the concept of adult development and the idea that the individual evolves throughout his life by crossing thresholds of his own consciousness as well as being conscious of his environment. This growth is only possible in the natural or voluntary acquisition of new mental models useful for the meaning of life experience.

Emotional intelligence is a useful tool for fighting stress at work:

- We can learn how to develop it.

- It responds to individual issues of emotional regulation.
- It takes into account relational dynamics; the role played in the quality of interactions and the effects of organization on psychic functioning.

WHAT TO EXPECT FROM EMOTIONAL INTELLIGENCE IN STRESS MANAGEMENT?

The development of emotional intelligence will have immediate effects on how an individual confronts a stressful situation. The ability not to identify oneself with one's emotion, to be able to label it, to take note of one's presence but not to be overwhelmed, offers possibilities of self-regulation which fight against the disorganizing effects of stress.

However, it must not be the only contribution we expect. The risk would be to put stress responsibility on each separately. However, organizational effects are a significant part of the stress felt by individuals at the professional level.

Emotional intelligence must be a central component of the corporate culture. Without necessarily being named as such, the dimensions of benevolence, authenticity, listening, trust, which are fundamental to effective relationships, are all structured on the skills related to emotional intelligence.

Therefore, if leaders and managers invest in their own personal growth, they improve their understanding of themselves and are thereby more available to each other. The values put forward are then modified to support a better relationship climate and reduce the stress felt by allowing better access to available resources.

You can achieve success by reducing the desertion and personal dissatisfaction that arises in the workplace via: career guidance. In this section on online psychology, we will explore the relationship between emotional intelligence and career guidance.

What is career guidance?

Career counseling, while not a clear concept, can be considered as "helping to choose a career, preparing for it, accessing it along with developing and progressing in a career.

29

Career counseling is intended to help the person develop a proper concept of himself and his role in the work. It is not a specific process, but continuous in time, which aims to improve the person as a goal.

In this perspective, career counseling is a complex and continuous process that seeks to create professional interests through self-knowledge, adapting those interests to the work competence of the subject, and assessing the needs of the job market, that is, engaging in the social work context.

If this conceptual representation is not enough to recognize the direct relationship between career counseling and emotional intelligence, it is because we have lost the original path and hoped that little but enough quality would allow our adolescents to reach the goal of being satisfied and successful professionals.

What do young people care about when they choose a career?

But we need to get closer to our reality. Are teenagers interested in getting involved in a professional program? Recent research in this area concludes, despite the career guidance process, that the final career decision depends mostly on the following elements:

- The career is socially acceptable;
- The career is economically viable;
- Moreover, it is easy and fast to enter the work area without considering the vocation; and,
- If it's the most straightforward subjects or the ones you like the most in high school, it's better.

So something happens that escapes our good intentions. Do we exclude personal education as an integral part of career guidance? Or do we act as if they are two different and parallel processes?

Emotional intelligence, the basis of self-knowledge

The individual work of self-knowledge—It is the inexhaustible source of resources for personal, family, academic and, of course, professional improvement. The teenager needs to know the interests, abilities, and expectations they have ahead of the future, as well as his fears, and this knowledge makes it more evident who they are and who they want to be.

Without this first individual work, the second instance of the process falls on deaf ears: the opportunities offered by higher education and the knowledge of the reality of work and the environment in which it is located. In general, it is this second instance that gains more weight during the specific career counseling process, without considering that its success depends on the self-awareness and emotional maturity of the adolescent.

However, the numbers show there are few counseling professionals who have a real opportunity to cover the entire process, especially if it is treated as specific during the diversified cycle. Therefore, we need to draw on other trends, technologies, strategies, methodologies and proposals that allow us to move closer to the duty of career advice by incorporating this into our work on "Emotional Intelligence" as art and part of the process of choosing a career.

The philosopher Pascal once wrote more than 300 years ago: "Nothing is more powerful than an idea whose time has come." Well, Emotional Intelligence is an idea whose time has come.

Emotional intelligence is a way of interacting with a world that takes into account feelings and includes skills such as impulse control, self-awareness, motivation, enthusiasm, perseverance, empathy, mental agility, and more. They configure character traits such as self-discipline, compassion, or altruism; these are indispensable prerequisites for productive and creative social adaptation. This concept is increasingly valued around the world, with a pronounced impact on the workplace.

This ability to live and handle emotions is learned since childhood. For this reason, the family is the school where the child learns to develop his emotional intelligence. But parents do not always know how important it is to address, integrate, and control the emotions of children. The children of families in which emotions are well cared for are friendlier and better students, though their "other" intelligence, logic, is not brilliant.

Family and school are fundamental. When developing emotional intelligence, it is never too late to make corrections and acquire new skills in the field. We play a lot, and know no matter if we are youngsters, adolescents, or adults, we can always develop a more productive area of emotions. Success in decision-making depends heavily on the maturity and emotional stability of the person deciding.

Kinds of emotional intelligence

With the development of this discipline, they have identified different types of emotional intelligence:

a. Intrapersonal intelligence is considered the ability of the individual to understand and recognize one's emotions as well as to know how to move around them subjectively. Once the person knows their emotional dimension, they have better and better control over their lives, which leads to more stability and decision-making.

b. The other dimension of emotional functioning is interpersonal. It refers to the ability of the individual to understand and act on other people's emotions. The individual becomes an enhancement of intellectual resources because, by controlling his emotional functioning, he achieves fundamental added value in his decision-making and problem-solving performance.

c. In this sense, the five components of the emotional coefficient agree with it; three are person-related abilities (self-knowledge, self-control, and self-motivation) or so-called intrapersonal intelligence. And the other two about other people (who know others' feelings and know about assertiveness), whom we call Interpersonal Intelligence.

Self-confidence is knowing your own emotions. Self-control is the ability to change or stop feelings to avoid life situations being a problem. And self-motivation, i.e., the ability of individuals to stimulate themselves in adverse circumstances.

The two remaining components of the emotional coefficient, which relate to the ability to know other persons (interpersonal intelligence), refer to the skills to understand the emotional state of others who at the time offer advantageous skills and skills with others to interact; and, finally, it is the ability to assert oneself, that is, the ability to be prompt in situations, either with actions or words.

Decision Making

Finally, the last key of the process comes into play: decision-making. Throughout this whole approach, I have identified the essential elements of the career guidance process: Self-knowledge, which we will call Emotional Intelligence from now on. Professional information, which in the second instance plays the most crucial role in vocational guidance, which is regularly practiced in high school; and not least the necessary result of the two previous successful and satisfactory decisions.

Decisions understood as the choice of a procedure-specific are vital because they depend on the success of a business, a career, the fate of a person, a country, etc.

There is at least one classic optimization theory in decision making where we are not sure the counselor deals with such information and tries to put it into practice in the career counseling process, but instead lists the natural steps we will use to establish a relationship between the three main elements of vocational guidance already mentioned. These steps, according to Tarter (1998), are:

- Identify the problem, that is, identify the discrepancies between the current situation and the desired results.
- Diagnose the problem or collect and analyze the information that explains the nature of the problem.
- Define the alternatives, i.e., develop all potential solutions.
- Investigate the consequences of what would happen if...? Anticipate the likely effects of each alternative.
- Decide to Assess and choose the best alternative that maximizes the achievement of the goals.
- Then do it, make the decision, or implement it.

According to the previous approach, the first two steps of the decision-making process must necessarily be the first instance of the guidance processor, as we call it, the identification of my emotional intelligence potentials and weaknesses essential to self-knowledge. The stimulation of the five elements of emotional IQ is the key to working and training the students in this case.

Use standardized psychological tests. It can be a resource that helps the student to assess his / her abilities and balance his / her interests. All of this will be effective if we do not forget to resort to considerations, to transfer that information to the actual situation of the student, and to relate those results to the information already given about the person as a human being and what he wants in terms of himself and those around him. Psychological tests are not wrong in themselves; they are insufficient because we do not adequately use the results they achieve.

The third step or definition of alternatives corresponds to the second element or the second instance of the professional process: the search for other options or study opportunities at a higher level. As we know, this should include all available information on specialized and professional work and begin to reject those options that by their nature do not match the results of the first instance.

The Fourth Natural Decision-Making Step - Examine the Consequences. It again poses the problem of self-knowledge, so Emotional Intelligence returns here to play a superior role. The confidence in myself and my potential, self-control, not to guide decisions by impulse and one's first impression; In addition to the ability to survive, though I have not found any quick and appropriate answers, the competences I have to test at this stage of the process.

This fourth step gradually brings me to the fifth, pick the best alternatives, and then set off: prepare for entrance exams, review and update documents, make pre-registration, and so forth. Confront yourself with the reality and perform actions that enable you to achieve what you intended to do. Success will undoubtedly be the practical result of this long journey.

More tips for combining emotional intelligence with career guidance

Because Emotional Intelligence can be cultivated and fully identified with Career Counseling, consider the following factors in your daily work, both individually and in groups:

- Empathy. Opening up to others. Watch and listen. Look at the other person's gestures, his look, and his way of speaking. Learn to feel what you feel.
- Cultivate self-control without suppressing emotions. Encourage observation and analysis of how these

feelings work for something. Or if they hurt.

- Use this opportunity to offer to analyze their tensions and instincts. Order and direct them without being displaced.
- Rewind. Ask after a dispute or a sad day if your reaction was proportionate and whether it was worth behaving so.
- They are looking for opportunities to laugh. Laughter and good humor make us happier. And statistics say that they prolong life.

The question of paradigms. What could you do in your school if you were to do it today, would you dramatically change the process of career guidance to an assertive and learning-promoting process? This is a question everyone must answer based on their experience and practice in their institution. It puts us at the limit of our paradigm.

What I do not do right now, if I did it, would it significantly improve my work? Answering this question of honesty and the obligation to work as a counselor for the change that brings the answer is an exercise in emotional and rational intelligence. Do it a challenge and to commit to a possible reality that would benefit all.

CHAPTER 2
EMOTIONAL INTELLIGENCE IN THE DAILY LIFE

For years, we have been listening to the term for emotional intelligence, coined by psychologist Daniel Goleman. But what is Emotional Intelligence that we all understand? And how can we apply it to our everyday lives??

Emotional intelligence is the ability to understand our feelings and those of others together and to solve our everyday problems without the world coming upon us. Emotional intelligence is the ability to handle emotions.

Why should we have more emotional intelligence? If we had to summarize it in a few words, maybe we could say it's so we can be happier. What is the meaning of life if we do not try to be satisfied? Problems will indeed come, and life will not always smile at us, but if we want to we have the power to be happier.

And how does it work? Develop our emotional intelligence. We are learning to deal with our emotions with ourselves and with others. Taking responsibility for them and being aware that we are the ones who can direct them to affect our well-being or discomfort.

Ideas to Sharpen Your Emotional Intelligence Day By Day

Next, we offer you some ideas you can put into practice daily to develop your emotional intelligence in the field. Dare, and start doing it! You will be surprised by the benefits:

- **Be motivated to improve emotionally:** We will not change unless we do our part. Nobody can help us to quit smoking, lose weight, etc. if we have no predisposition to do so. The same happens in emotional intelligence. And there is a saying that says, "Do more, who wants, than who can."
- **Learn to keep the small setbacks from day to day:** Look for the positive side of everything that happens to you. Have you lost the love, the work, or a friend? Do not worry too much, you can think that these are bad times, but everything happens, and that life will surprise you with new possibilities.

- **Do not torture yourself with negative thoughts:** The entry into the spiral of negative feelings does not help us at all. Really, what do you solve with negative thoughts? Try to learn to say "enough." Put on music, dance, exercise, talk to others, distract your mind when it becomes "stupid."
- **If you feel bad, go to someone who brings you peace and refuge**: Surely you have someone nearby who, if you feel bad, can see life as being positive. Look for her, look for her words, and thank her for her friendship.
- **Be open with others:** Be sensitive. Do not censor others so much; try to understand them, to pretend others are the way you want them is a senseless war. Take the positive side of the people. We all have shortcomings as well as virtues.
- **Listen to your body; it will help you to recognize many of your feelings:** Did you have a knot in your stomach when you got bad news? Do you feel dizzy in the face of this new situation? Find out how your body is the first to recognize

emotions and help yourself to understand, even transform. Learn to breathe, calm down, etc.

- **Do not take things "so personally":** If we stop thinking a little, we are in step, why shouldn't we do our part and try to make things more relaxed? That the boss today is unbearable, is his thing, do not let yourself be influenced. You don't like the new person who joined your gang? Do not let it break your friendship with the rest, let it be.
- **Solve conflicts with others positively:** They say it is best when people are understood. So, if you have a problem with someone, try to solve it in the best possible way, show dialogues and points of view. If you feel that you are a negative person, and you cannot "walk away," sing quietly.

So, if you want to be happy, all you need is the desire and the effort that, together with these tips, will lead you to see life differently. Train your emotional intelligence and discover its benefits in everyday life, both for yourself and your relationships with others.

Two Essential Concepts: Positive Psychology and Emotional Intelligence

This notion of the human persona, which is more in the realm of philosophical investigation and discussion, has an impact on the purely theoretical. At that time, the enlightened vision led to significant political and social changes that have been proven in every history book, and along with them, a tremendous scientific and industrial advance that has skyrocketed in a few decades and whose benefits and consequences we still live today.

It is enough to observe life in every big city, especially in industrialized countries, as always fast and flexible. The need for efficiency and effectiveness as well as personal and social success, transforming social relations of new technologies and social networks.

Where a deep reflection comprises no more than 140 characters or more than a few hours will take as much or where the vision that a person has changed according to their Facebook status; to overcome the need to be a Separatist by entering the supply and demand market in love. Which is more based on sentimentality and, unfortunately, on sex appeal?

The change in the understanding of the concept of traditional equality that kept the Christian worldview to a particular position of equilibrium. It is not the same, but with inherent differences that distinguish us and after that, we were looking for drive, but where equality is synonymous with identity. Numerous authors have studied and written about the consequences of today's society: Frankl, Fromm, Goleman, and others.

Recognize yourself

Given this reality before the world in which we live, psychology has decided to return to a fundamental principle: Know thyself. As old as the oracles of Delphi from where the legend says that it originated and is always essential because man is still the same beyond changing his social and historical circumstances. This old and ever-new saying has today been translated into so-called emotional intelligence, which can be broadly defined as "the ability to understand how one perceives, understands and manages one's emotions."

Emotions are therefore not understood as something extrinsic to man, but as an integral part of the whole, which can enter into the realm of reason and consequently be channeled for the good of the person and society. This means emotions are not enemies to suppress or control, but rather a path of development that can be trained and grasped so that the person can fully exploit them and not just have another life — healthy and harmonious, but also have the ability to face the adversities that arise in it.

The path to emotional intelligence

Getting the most out of people is perhaps one of the most laudable and noble things psychology does today. Since psychological science as such began to adjust, special attention was always paid to what was wrong with man: mental disorders, the unconscious, and the Freudian theory. The vision we still have of psychology is in many places, even that of a madman and is in some ways promoted by mass media.

Emotional intelligence is one of those new trends in which the focus is more fixated on what we do about the positive evaluation of emotions, the search for happiness, and its realization, love, strengths, and virtues. Some of the new areas in which psychology wants to help people include helping them to reach their set goals.

How to recognize the emotional intelligence

You probably have never asked yourself such questions before. But dealing with emotional intelligence can undoubtedly lead to one or the other Aha-knowledge.

Here are six features that suggest emotional intelligence.

Look at your circle of acquaintances, in your work environment. To which persons do these characteristics apply? Maybe they apply to you too? Then you can assume that you or these persons have high emotional intelligence!

Usually people with emotional intelligence presents such characteristics:

- High control their emotions: they are well able to influence and control their moods and feelings. This often happens through inner dialogue. In this way, they can more easily manage their emotions when needed than a person with a lower EQ. This is an advantage, for example, when they are angry, or they do not want to show their disappointment. People with high emotional intelligence are not so exposed to their feelings. The ability to have self-control, that is, to respond appropriately to the situation, proves to be advantageous both in professional and private life.

- They are able to motivate other people: who has a high level of emotional intelligence can more easily drive themselves in difficult life situations according to the associated requirements. This makes it possible for them to repeatedly develop their willingness to perform and to be enthusiastic about a particular cause. This ability to self-motivate is particularly needed in stressful situations, e.g. for example, if a specific project develops differently than initially planned or desired.

- They have strong social skills: people with high emotional intelligence quickly find contact with their fellow human beings. It is also easy for them to uphold and maintain relationships over a more extended period.

- They have a realistic image of themselves: people with high EQ can assess themselves thoroughly. They know their own needs, identify their feelings as well as their goals, and the motives for their actions. In other words, you are self-confident. They are "self-aware" of their abilities, strengths, weaknesses, and feelings.

Habits That People With High Emotional Intelligence Have And That You Can Also Have

1 Recognize their feelings and those of others

They have a broad emotional vocabulary that helps them know how to express exactly how they feel and put it into words. Also, they have what we would call "empathy," that is, they can put themselves in the shoes of the other person and feel what the different feels like. They recognize the expressions and nonverbal language of other people and can interpret what they think and get all the possible information from it.

2 Express your emotions and thoughts correctly

By recognizing one's emotions and feelings, it is easier for them to know what they have to do or how they have to behave. In this sense, they express their emotions and their thoughts more honestly with themselves and with others. They don't silence their feelings, they listen to them, and know what each passion means in each context. They know how to regulate the intensity of their feelings and express them in the right way, just as they want. They are the owners of their emotional expression, not mere fighters at the mercy of their runaway emotions.

3 They are healthy and do not get offended easily

People with high emotional intelligence are characterized by having a firm personality and not taking too much comment from others. Threats are not carried personally, and they know how to differentiate between facts and opinions. They separate the constructive criticisms from the criticisms that only intend to sink them and know how to get away from derogatory comments that only bring destruction. They know how to distinguish between attacks and how they react to those attacks and can decide to react in the least painful way for themselves.

4 Focus on the positive, even on adversity

Highly intelligent people are emotionally aware of their surroundings and do not focus too much time on the negative. They prefer to keep the focus on the positives of each situation, even when they have problems. They practice dissociation and see the status from different points of view so they can find a solution. They do not get overwhelmed with the difficulties and sink, but instead put all their energies into what they can do to solve the situation, whatever depends on them and that they have under control. In the face of all difficulties, there is something positive to focus on.

5 Happy people with good vibes surround them

"Tell me who you are with, and I will tell you who you are" is something that shows people with high emotional intelligence are cheerful, so they relate to dreamy people, optimistic people, and positive energy. They move away from toxic people and energetic vampires who want to drag them into their negative view of life. By having good vibes and surrounding themselves with positive people, they see the world from a healthier perspective that favors creativity. They usually relate to people who are good influences and who complete them.

CHAPTER 3
PERSONALITY, EMOTIONS AND RESILIENCE

We are each as we are, just as no one is what he was, that is clear. But have you ever wondered how much your way of being influences how you feel or that more positive or negative emotions appear in your life? To what extent does your personality influence the inclination of this scale?

If we are happy, our mental health will be better; we will feel greater subjective well-being, and our satisfaction with life will be higher. Finding out if your personality traits make your happiness is greater or, if on the contrary, cause negative emotions to predominate in your life!

Why is positive affect beneficial?

Positive affect is the propensity to experience more positive than negative emotions over time. These pleasant emotions make people have a repertoire of behaviors broader and they are more productive than those who feel more emotional discomfort. Also, it promotes healthy lifestyle habits, making it an effective means of preventing bad health.

This makes satisfaction with life higher. This satisfaction is the perception that each one of us has of the quantity and quality of happiness that we enjoy. But how important is this in our well-being? A lot. And not only on a psychological level but on a physical level. High satisfaction with life is related to a higher life expectancy, health, and longevity.

It supposes an advantage in the hormonal balance, as well as in other indicators of both the physiological and immune systems. But it is also associated with greater satisfaction with our social relationships and with our salary and job. Finally, it gives us adaptive coping strategies, aimed at solving problems.

Personality and happiness

Numerous studies have been carried out on how personality traits influence the type of emotions that predominate in our lives. Thus, it has been found that neuroticism is related to negative affectivity, while extraversion is related to positive affectivity. In other words, introverted people tend to score higher in negative affect and those who are extraverted in a positive effect.

Now let's look at the different types of proficient personalities. We found four. The first is encompassed by self-constructing people, who score high on positive affect and low on negative. This first type, as is logical, presents more elevated levels of happiness or subjective well-being.

The second type of personality is affective-high. It would be those people with intense affection, both towards the positive pole and towards the negative pole. They are the next happiest. The third type follows them: the low effective, which is those who present low levels of both types of affections.

Finally, the least happy would be those of the self-destructive affective personality type. These people have low levels of positive affectivity, but high levels of negative affectivity. That said, it is not difficult to imagine that your subjective well-being levels are the lowest.

Personality and resilience

In these investigations, it has been found that the auto-constructive type presents high scores in extraversion and low scores in neuroticism. But not only that, they also get high scores on another feature that we have not mentioned so far: responsibility.

This personality profile is not only related to higher levels of happiness but is also associated with greater resilience: the ability to see difficulties as challenges to be overcome and from which to emerge reinforced, instead of seeing them as insurmountable walls or threats.

Thus, people who are not able to cope with situations fit the vulnerable or inhibited profile. Or what is the same: with the self-destructive type. Given this, it can be assumed that the personality has a strong relationship with our global health, influencing the different areas of our life, such as our emotional state, with all that this means.

In real terms, resilience is the ability that an object has to return to its initial state after applying an external force that modifies it. This is what happens, for example, when we squeeze a rubber ball in our hand and suddenly stop doing it.

In the 50s of the last century, the term resilience began to be used in the field of humanities, to describe the quality of the human being, which makes him able to overcome adversity effectively. Today we know that this quality is composed of a biological, psychological and social role.

Surely you have ever heard of resilience, such as the ability that some people have to overcome the various circumstances that life has in store for them. We all know someone who, in the face of a traumatic event such as the death of a loved one, recovers and uses his resources to move forward with an admirable gesture. It is a resilient person. And, every person who meets these characteristics directly shares the pillars of resilience, some basic concepts that help each person in some way to overcome adversity, to face the tragic event.

Discover what are the six pillars of resilience and their meaning

Self-knowledge

It is essential, to overcome the traumas, which we know each other well, that we look within ourselves and understand what emotions arise in each moment and how to manage those emotions. To do this, practicing self-knowledge and spending time with yourself will help you in each of those moments. So you know, the most crucial resilience pillar is the knowledge we have of ourselves because it helps us measure how each situation affects us.

Motivation

The second pillar of resilience is motivation. Because it is the primary weapon for anyone, who wants to move on. Working motivation will be essential to continue after a hard blow. It is necessary that when we want something, we can visualize it and draw up a plan to carry out what we want. We will have to lay the foundations, both long-term, and short term, enjoying the rewards of our effort along the way.

Independence

To be resilient, we have to use our weapons. This does not mean that we cannot ask for help when we need it, but that we do not have to delegate our effort to other people. Remember that if you want to get ahead, you will have to do it yourself, and even if there are people you can rely on, the main job should be yours.

Responsibility

Resilient people take responsibility for their own lives. Indeed, sometimes, we do not deserve the things that happen to us, the circumstances are unfair, and the facts are devastating, but the truth is that the responsibility to overcome is only ours. If we do not understand this and take responsibility for our well-being, we will not advance in our personal development because we will not have the capacity to be resilient.

Optimism

The ability to see the right side of things is another of the fundamental pillars of resilience, and that is, without confidence, we can't move forward in the most stringent circumstances. The truth is that everything wrong has its positive side, we can learn from everything and, when we learn to see it, the road becomes much more pleasant and encouraging.

Humor

Humor is something resilient people have in common. Taking things with a laugh can help to dramatize situations and give them another point of view, so getting ahead can be more natural and of course, more fun.

We tend to perceive a negative emotion as something to avoid and even believe that if we do, it will disappear. However, this is not so. The key is to learn to manage them.

Popular wisdom often advises avoiding and even suppressing negative emotions. The less they show themselves, the better and the less they experience them too. They say they don't do us that much good.

Fear, anger, resentment, shame, or guilt are not welcome. They are frowned upon. And although getting rid of what does not suit us is, in principle, advisable, it is not so much to ignore or repress it. Negative emotions must be expressed, this is to release them, but without being carried away by them, otherwise, they may end up mastering our behavior.

If you know you shouldn't take something because it can hurt you, don't do it. Now, emotions don't work that way; It is not so easy to avoid them without obtaining negative consequences. Suppressing negative emotions has a high price.

What happens to the dust when you accumulate it under the carpet?

Imagine that your negative emotions are a thin or thick layer of dust on the floor. If you sweep up the sand and hide it under the carpet, the dirt will not be visible at first, and you can live a healthy life without you or anyone else noticing it. You know it's under the rug, but since you do not see it, it probably will not bother you.

The days go by, and every time dust appears, you hide it under the rug. Thus, every day, there is more and more of it. You know, but as you do not see it, you probably decide to act as if nothing has happened.

How long do you think you can hide the fact that under the carpet hides a layer of increasingly thick dust? Would it take time to highlight everything you have hidden there? Do you think this can cause you to stumble on that mountain in which your carpet has become?

Accumulating negative emotions, such as the dust you hide under your carpet, only delays the inevitable. In one way or another, these emotions will finally manifest themselves, and they can even do everything together in an explosive way.

In the end, in most cases, you are probably in a situation where you have to deal with these emotions in one way or another.

Emotions are not hidden, they are managed

Emotions are a vital part of our daily lives. You are happy because you see something fun, or you get frustrated, for example, by the traffic; the ups and downs that you may encounter can significantly affect your well-being.

Also, your ability to regulate emotions can have an impact on how people around you see you. First of all, remember that depending on how you evaluate your experiences, you will react emotionally and that some of them do not require special regulation, as long as they are adapted to the situation in which they were lived.

For example, expressing anger can help you feel better, but it's usually not appropriate or unusually adaptive in many cases. It's about finding a way to free yourself from acceptance, respect, and calm.

Removing negative emotions is not a good idea, it is advisable to learn to manage them, that is to say, to give them the floor and regulate them.

How To Control Negative Emotions

Being able to influence your thoughts and emotions increases confidence in your ability to cope with them. To begin, to manage a negative emotion, you must start by selecting a situation in which it occurs and tries to avoid the circumstances that trigger it.

Other times, the solution is to avoid certain people in certain circumstances or find a way to calm down and see that state of peace of mind before facing the threatening situation.

The secret is to identify the situation or circumstance in the first place and the negative emotion that would be triggered.

The next step is to modify the situation: Once identified, try to modify it in such a way that the conditions that trigger negative emotions do not occur. Keep in mind this change must be born from you. For example, you may have to change your expectations in the face of the situation, reduce the demands, or use a loving, comprehensive, and empathetic look.

It will be helpful to change your attention focus. That is to say: instead of focusing on what you already know triggers your negative emotions, look at other aspects that are to your liking. Try not to focus so much on what you dislike and look for what makes you feel good, something for which you can be grateful.

Another point you can keep in mind to control your negative emotions is to change your thoughts. These are the center of our deepest feelings; the place where the beliefs that drive them live. Keep in mind that by changing your dreams, you may not be able to change the situation, but at least you can change the way you think the situation is affecting you.

Finally, you can try to change your responses to your negative emotions. If your emotional management mechanisms do not work and arise out of control, the final step in emotional regulation is to try to control the response. This will help you not to suppress negative emotions because it will push you to regulate them.

For this, something useful is to identify the physical sign that gives way to that emotion is triggered. Acting on that gesture or reaction will help you control the response. This could be achieved through actions as simple as deep breathing or closing your eyes, which, in turn, is often useful for managing anger.

Remember that the emotions are yours and, therefore, you are the most responsible for managing them. The final responsibility for your behavior belongs to you, and that is why it is essential to be aware that no one is as guilty of how you respond emotionally as yourself.

CHAPTER 4
THE EMOTIONAL DEVELOPMENT OF KIDS

Emotions accompany us in our daily lives by being the fundamental support of our relationships and our knowledge of ourselves. Knowing how emotional development occurs in the early years of our lives is essential to understanding and educating children in their well-being. Let's talk about it.

What is emotional development?

Emotional development is a complex concept that involves a large number of aspects such as the emergence of emotions, their expression, their consciousness, and their regulation in others and ourselves. Moreover, this process is, in turn, is linked to both cognitive and social development, feeding each other with great force, as well as language development.

Children experience sensations related to elemental and primitive aspects from birth. The new world is, therefore based on very primary emotional parameters based on its needs and necessary actions. It is only with time and through interaction with the environment that we will be able to shape the emotional impact we all have.

Although the exact moments when different types of emotions appear are not yet established, everything seems to indicate that it is necessary to wait ten months before children show the full range of the basic emotions known: joy, fear, sadness, anger, surprise and disgust, which progressively develops according to their cerebral maturation. However, it should be noted that this may vary depending on the occurrence of particular circumstances, according to the researchers.

Moreover, at the level of emotional expression, although babies indeed present different types of facial expressions such as interest, disgust or discomfort, these do not necessarily have to be adapted to the situation or the stimulus that provokes them. But it is essential to emphasize the value of the communication they imply, which stand out as signals regulating the behavior of attachment figures to meet the needs of children. For example, crying in addition to embarrassment, parents must feed their babies, keep them company, or try to eliminate the cause of their pain.

It is not before two months that babies learn to differentiate emotional expressions, although they do not necessarily respond to their emotional significance. However, between the fourth and seventh months, they are already able to associate it with the appropriate emotion.

Thus, with growth, emotions are socialized, their expression is reinforced and more complex emotions such as pride at 24 months or guilt and envy between 3 and four years are start emerging.

The symbolic game stage

One of the most important emotional development events is when children develop the ability to play symbolically after two years, as they learn to represent both their emotional states and those of others. That is, the child is already able to understand that the other person is different from himself and can begin to put himself in his place as a support for the development of the capacity for empathy.

The bond of attachment

Children present from birth the need to be emotionally supported by others. We thus find their innate predisposition for the construction of the relationship of affection. The bond between the baby and the caregiver, which helps them to feel safe and protected when it occurs healthily, without rejection, and without ambivalent behavior.

Moreover, it is the attachment relationship that provides an opportunity to begin to understand because it is configured as the privileged context where babies can learn to express, interpret, and share their experiences. They learn emotions through different interactions with their primary caregiver, which will influence the establishment of future relationships.

The importance of emotional education

However, it is not only essential to know what the process of psychological development is, but also how we can help to improve it so children can more easily manage their own emotions and become emotionally literate adults.

At present, the resumption of emotion research has deepened their development and functionality to offer new perspectives in the field of education, one of which is emotional education.

Emotional competence in children: This is how parents can promote emotional development

Emotional competence is essential for a peaceful coexistence

There are many different social skills. These include, for example: contacting other people, motivating others to find solutions together, mutual appreciation, involving people, but also recognizing problems and finding a solution together.

Under emotional competence in children, we understand learned skills and attitudes that are conducive to peaceful coexistence. However, these are not measurable, such as mathematical skills or knowledge in fields such as physics or chemistry. Nevertheless, safe handling of one's own emotions, as well as empathy is of enormous importance for the future emotional, private, and professional life of your child.

Developmental disorders are challenging to recognize themselves

Developmental disorders do not always have recognizable causes but can have a profoundly negative impact on children's social and emotional skills. There are many factors involved, such as heredity, nutrition, or social interaction. Also, there are numerous developmental disorders with different degrees of severity. A general provision is therefore hardly possible.

Only in direct comparison to peers is a developmental disorder recognizable. If you have a suspicion, you should have your pediatrician issue a referral for a psychologist.

A developmental disorder should be treated accordingly

Developmental disorders generally have an unfavorable prognosis. But with modern therapy and new medication, the symptoms can be minimized as much as possible. However, complete recovery rarely occurs.

In an actual developmental disorder of the child, it is vital that you adequately deal with the disease to respond appropriately to the behavior of your child. Plans to promote the child should be developed and implemented with the attending physician, as far as your child's options are concerned. Further information on developmental dysfunctions can be found here.

Pay attention to the signals

When a baby receives a lot of loving care right from the start, it is already sensitized to its feelings. Therefore, the most important tip is: Be sensitive, pay attention to the child's signals, and react quickly and appropriately.

All emotions are allowed

Children can show emotions, both positive and negative. And every child is allowed to do that in his way, whether loud or quiet. Everyone is angry sometimes. Make it clear to your child that this emotion is natural and you value the child, but that aggressive behavior is not right and that you have to learn how to direct your anger so you do not hurt or damage any other person.

Take Feelings Seriously

Children want to be taken seriously with their feelings. For smaller or larger disasters, they are not as much about things as we adults are. Avoid playing down your child's sentiments: "Do not pretend!"

Parents are role models

Even in the emotional world, the little ones learn from the big ones. Therefore, parents are allowed to show their children feelings and explain them in an age-appropriate way. They do not let you imagine anything anyway. On the other hand, it is scary for children when they feel something is in the air and we do not initiate it. Parents are just as immune to inappropriate outbursts of anger as children. Then it is essential to apologize afterward.

CHAPTER 5
EMOTIONAL INTELLIGENCE AND SELF-ESTEEM

Self-esteem is the sense of self-worth that manifests through self-acceptance and self-esteem, motivation, treatment with dignity, and self-love. This sense of value is the pillar on which our happiness as a human rests. It is therefore important to have an adequate level of self-esteem so that the person can develop as such, because he recognizes himself as the owner of himself, his body and all that he contains, of his mind, including his ideal, his thoughts, his emotions, that he is, a limited being without forgetting the possibilities, whose happiness depends on him and nobody else.

Each person must try to properly develop those emotional skills that allow him to grow as a person and with a level of self-esteem sufficient for his personal development and success. However, some people experience constant emotional blockages that prevent them from adequately performing their abilities in different scenes of daily life, which makes them feel bad about themselves and not be satisfied with the development of their lives.

We all have unresolved feelings even if we are not aware of them, and these feelings can take many forms: hating oneself, anxiety attacks, sudden mood swings, guilt, exaggerated reactions, hypersensitivity, finding the negative side of the situations and feeling helpless, all that make us experience a decline in self-esteem.

Undoubtedly, the social and family context exerts a particular influence on us until we become, on some occasions, the product of what the other person says or thinks of us, the messages we have received since childhood become flesh and in adulthood our self is shaped by what others think I am, what I think others think I am and what I really want to be.

Devaluation itself is also a product of comparison with others, we perceive the other in the flatness of their attributes, and I compare myself to it, I lose this comparison, and I feel it in inferior conditions. In short, our categories are developed in the evolutionary plot of our life, and are related to our social and personal experiences.

Anyone with low self-esteem can produce a false identity that protects himself from the confusion and disorientation caused by internalized shame. When he feels helpless and underrated, he begins to hide what he feels and thinks of as a strategy. This mask with which it is presented to the world can take different forms by which this person claims, asks in an unsatisfied way, a recognition of the other.

Emotional intelligence also postulates the treatment of emotions, that is to say, the ability to control impulses to adapt them to an objective. For a person with low self-esteem, it would be a question of changing the low-value emotions felt at a given moment, of learning how to manage them, of working on them and, if possible, of suppressing them or adapt them to a specific environment or moment.

Learning to create a particular emotional state is essential, for which someone with low self-esteem is recommended to start by trying to control the duration of their emotions. They begin by identifying the feeling (or passion) of sadness, and then decide if they can or should control it and other harmful emotions.

On the other hand, emotions put us in motion, and it concerns the ability to self-motivate, to develop the ability to get down and dirty about what we have to do to be able to wear it in the best possible way, by soothing other impulses that divert us from the task of improving the performance of any business activity.

This additional postulate of emotional intelligence, adapted to the issue of low self-esteem, would mean that the person experiencing a situation of low self-esteem should be a motivated person, capable of performing a given task or of being motivated to continue their daily life without being affected by the comments or attitudes of others, driving themselves each day of their life, to achieve goals, dreams, and their ideal life.

Finally, there is the management of emotions. The skills described above can be used in different ways once developed. In case of low self-esteem, a person who identifies his or her negative feelings, whatever they are, and manages or self-controls them, and who can motivate himself, can improve his relationships in the same way that others can.

The person who does this will not depend on others, but on himself. To do this, it usually requires a lot of work, time, and making good decisions. However, if we teach people to adapt their emotions, to control them, whether positive or negative, constructive or destructive, and to uniquely identify them, and be less damaging to themselves, then the can live with less stress.

Therefore, the author assures that adequate emotional or assertive education could prevent some emotional issues or poor self-esteem. However, the first step in managing emotions is to identify them. So, if you have negative emotions that can cause you to feel bad about yourself, you need to start with an excellent emotional education, and good emotional intelligence to help prevent low self-esteem.

How to gain confidence with emotional intelligence

The emotional mind feeds the intelligent with deeper feelings and convictions. The rational thought that is more intellectual refines the actions you take in your daily life. But, since nothing is perfect, these two minds also go into crisis. The rational cannot always impose itself, but most of the time, it vetoes the inflow of emotions that may displease us.

The three pillars of trust in yourself

Knowing how to earn more trust from the people around you. What's more, getting others to accept their ideas; getting more people's eyes is also an essential requirement of leadership. And once again, let's get to the point! According to Frances Frei, a Harvard professor, trust depends on three pillars.

- The 1st. It's how much you present yourself as real. Let's simplify it by by calling it: authenticity.
- The 2nd. It is the clarity of the rational arguments you use to defend your ideas. We can call it logic.
- The 3rd. And the last point is how much the person in front of you feels that you are mindful. Let's call it empathy.

Note that any oscillation in any of these three elements will surely shake the confidence you have in yourself. If your spirit is already threatened by someone, evaluate these three elements, and find out where you should be paying more attention. Review your placement here and plan the next steps to regain balance in your relationship. The good news is that if you decide to get started, you may already begin to convey much more confidence than you have been able to demonstrate to date.

Gesture like him

Notice how he moves his arms, where he places his hands, and where he directs his gaze. It is important that you pay attention to these small details and look for ways to do the same when you are in front of him. Each person has a mental map and a particular intelligence, some people like to move their hands a lot, touch you, "feel" with the touch of the conversation. Just like there are others who, on the contrary, are direct, do not move their arms. Well, if the person in front of you sees that you do the same as them, you will be familiar and will begin to build trust. But if on the contrary, she sees you as another "species" and different, the process may be slower or even impossible since if their fear gland is activated, they may flee.

Talk like him

In the oral expression there are also many cultural and personality traits, and that is why the person in front of you will seek to feel familiar with you and will verify that you speak the "same language," Try to align yourself with their expressions, it is possible it may be complicated at first, but over time you will discover how to talk with others. You do not have to release all your repertoire, but only that which is enough to build trust, wait to have passed this first barrier of faith to share your expressions and idioms.

Listen, listen and listen

It is essential to start out on the right foot, and nothing better than the other person see that what she says to you matters to you and that you are interested in the conversation. Try to make your first words with her always positive, a trick is to ask simple and straightforward questions that have definite answers. Make sure to use the "Yes or no" type of conversation, as this will make you breathe a collaborative atmosphere and the other person will be more willing in the future to respond with positive messages, i.e. "Do you find it interesting" or "Do you want coffee?"

CHAPTER 6
EMOTIONAL INTELLIGENCE AND RELATIONSHIPS

Nowadays it looks more and more that any relationship is likely to break and end. Infidelities, disappointments, and distancing hurt and are difficult to overcome.

It is hard to believe that "time heals all wounds" because all that one feels is that everything hurts and that nothing relieves the pain. Therefore, emotional intelligence is a resource for gradually closing these internal scars.

Finishing with something that made you feel loved and unique, and that also kept you in a "safe zone" is painful, but it's not healthy to stay in pain.

Being emotionally intelligent means that you can evaluate each situation from an agile point of view to act accordingly. In this way, you are not overcome by your thoughts and emotions because you control them.

Life is an unpredictable experience, and acting with emotional intelligence becomes a valuable resource for overcoming adversity. If you let the pain eat you up, you will often be caught in negative behavior and thought patterns. This can lead to psychological disorders such as depression or anxiety.

Listen to your body

Feeling knotted in the stomach when you arrive at the office can be a clue that your work is a source of stress. Feeling that your heart is pounding when you see that person you love can mean that you are in love. Listening to these feelings and underlying feelings will allow you to treat your emotions with reason.

Give your unconscious feelings

Try the free association. While you are relaxed, let your thoughts flow freely. Do not lose sight of them. Analyze your dreams. Keep a notebook and a pen next to your bed and write your goals as soon as you wake up, so you do not forget them. Pay special attention to dreams that are repeated or that are charged with strong emotions.

Write down your thoughts and feelings

Writing your thoughts and feelings can help in a meaningful way. A simple exercise like this could only take a few hours a week. This will help you to free your mind of everything that overwhelms you and will make you aware of negative and positive feelings.

Learn to distinguish when it's enough

There comes a time when you should stop looking inward and learn to change course. Keeping you on your negative thoughts will intensify them. Emotional intelligence involves not only the ability to search within oneself, but also to be present in the world around you.

TIPS TO HEAL YOUR EMOTIONS AFTER A BREAK

Ending a relationship is one of the most painful things that exist. It does not seem to be something we're going to die for, but it hurts. It hurts like it hurts when you are hit in the pit of your stomach. Like when someone closes the door very hard and catches your fingers. It is a sharp and constant pain, which is why it is essential to healing emotional wounds after a breakup with your partner because otherwise, your mood could get worse.

Even if they did not abandon you, even if the decision was yours because you consider it the best, the end also hurts. There is a void in you, and it will be necessary to heal your emotions by separating or taking your time. Emotions are one of the most precious things we have, and we have to deal with them.

Overcome the emotional pain of a break with these tips

And along the way, you will find many people who, with their good intentions, want to help. Let them tell you that you are better without him, that it was not for you or that it is not so much. These are tips that will have a significant impact on your self-esteem, even if they have good intentions.

It is true that time heals everything and that, sooner or later, you will eventually leave this stage of emotional suffering, and we give you some tips to cure this emotional pain after separation so that the treatment is cleaner. In this way, we will understand what we are going through, and we will make sure that we are well.

1- Take your time

In the process of emotional healing after a break, everyone takes time. Do not be overwhelmed by the desire to be healthy right away. It is normal to live a period of mourning. One of the things that influence our partner choice is the time that elapses between each love. If you hurry up and engage in another relationship, you will only hinder your healing.

You need to know that it is a moment that you permit yourself to feel bad. Of course, knowing that you will find yourself little by little better, that you will not stay forever in this situation. You already know if you want to heal your emotions after a breakup, it is necessary to understand that everyone has their time and that it is essential that you take yours.

2- Spend time with quality people

Although it is always important to choose people who add up, this is, even more, the case in such situations. When we meet people who make us feel good, they fill us with positive energy and make us feel at peace during the storm we are experiencing. This is one of the keys to healing the emotions of a broken heart, so do not miss it. Stay away from envious, jealous, or interested people. It does not matter that their plan is the most fun. Being with people who steal your energy will be the worst thing to do in this situation.

3- Get away from the excesses

Often, when we feel bad, we consume substances that make us feel better. It is human to want to avoid pain, and alcohol and drugs can momentarily anesthetize you. Remember that falling into these excesses will make you feel a lot worse later. This does not mean you cannot go out for a drink with friends, but if you abuse depressive substances the next day, your pain will be doubled. And that one, at best. At worst, you could fall into an addiction that would prolong your torture.

4- Learn difficult situations

You will surely have had other moments in life where you thought that your world was falling apart and that you moved forward despite that. These are situations that make us stronger and give us the tools to live more fully.

Whether we like it or not, ruptures are part of life and healing your broken heart will help you become a complete person and value our happiness more. Remember that other situations have come out, and you will leave as well.

Also, it will be right for you to stop and think about everything you learn about yourself and be proud of the path you take.

CHAPTER 7
EXERCISES TO DEVELOP EMOTIONAL INTELLIGENCE

To improve your emotional intelligence, you must unlearn certain aspects. Because beyond intellectual skills, there is undoubtedly this wisdom that emotions bring us.

Why is it so essential to improve your emotional intelligence? We face this area of our life that we should all develop and manage appropriately. To know how to listen, to understand the emotions of others, and to control oneself, to understand how to communicate, and to promote mutual respect where we all win is essential.

It is a type of intelligence that should be included in the school curriculum to develop these necessary skills in children from an early age. Emotional intelligence is, above all, a mode of self-knowledge, self-control, and expression. To know your own boundaries and at the same time, spot them before others. Avoid possible manipulations.

As we know, a high IQ is not always synonymous with happiness. The right intelligence, the one that promotes our well-being, our social relationships, and our professional success, is the one that relates to the emotional matters.

Exercises To Improve Your Emotional Intelligence

To Know oneself

To know oneself is an adventure that lasts a lifetime. It is an exercise that is carried out, day after day, marking our objectives and asking ourselves questions. It is an introspection task that we do each morning.

At night, analyze what you felt all day long. Have you acted as you wish? Have you spoken, defended according to your values? You can use a piece of paper, a newspaper, or your notebook. It is a straightforward exercise but at the same time illustrative. Ask yourself questions, find out about yourself, and clarify.

Emotional regulation

Think of your emotions as a balance. The key to well-being is in balance. Achieving this internal homeostasis requires adequate work which, according to Daniel Goleman, should focus on the following aspects:

Control your anger. When you notice that you are about to "fall" or "explode," visualize a small, quiet, airy room. It's your palace of thoughts.

Control your impulses. Before acting, think, reason, and analyze the situation.

Set your negative emotions. These states absorb our full attention by preventing any attempt to witness anything else.

Empathy to improve your emotional intelligence

Empathy is a concept we all know and appreciate, but we do not practice as much as we should. It is easier for us to put ourselves in the shoes of those who give us more positive feelings. We identify with them better, and the level of understanding and approach is more intense.

Now, why not try to empathize with more people who are bothering us? Try to put yourself in the other person's shoes, and you may discover what's behind it: insecurity, or low self-esteem.

This will allow us to manage our relationships better. This understanding and contact leads us to better decisions, to be more assured to understand the point of view of others.

Personal motivation

You do not feel like it today. You do not think like that. But from that moment, let's do a simple exercise: we'll look at the bright side, leaving the negative relegated. Get up every day thinking about something that you are passionate about and want to achieve. Set goals, short and long-term goals.

Life without illusion is not life. Find your daily motivation.

Sometimes, all insignificance is useful to us. End the day in this cafeteria where you have not yet entered. Call that person whom you have not seen for so long. Buy a new dress, plan a weekend getaway, sign up for a yoga or a painting class.

Social abilities

Try to communicate a little better, not only with words but also with gestures. Get close to your surroundings, draw a smile, offer a caress, a pat on the back, or a hug. You will see that the reaction of those around you is different.

Similarly, the art of social skills training requires strengthening the following aspects:

- Learn to listen, to express yourself, to communicate effectively.
- Train your assertiveness.
- Be respectful
- Practice compassion.
- Be patient.
- Use intuition, another essential tool to improve your emotional intelligence.

QUESTIONS TO KNOW MORE ABOUT EMOTIONAL INTELLIGENCE

Aristotle said that anyone could get angry since it is an easy thing. However, getting annoyed with the right person, in the right degree, at the right time, with the right purpose and in the right way is difficult. It all resides in emotional intelligence.

We talk about the proper management of our emotions and many other disturbances from which we are often caught.

We want to clarify some typical concepts of emotional intelligence and reflect on the subject.

1. What is emotional intelligence?

Mayer & Salovey (1997) were the first to define emotional intelligence from an academic-scientific point of view. In simple terms, we can define emotional intelligence, also abbreviated as EQ (Emotional Quotient) or IE (Emotional Intelligence) as the ability to integrate rational thinking (what we think) with emotions (what we feel) to make optimal decisions, taking into consideration what is important to us. In other words, it means being intelligent with emotions.

2. Why do you say train and not acquire? I don't think I'm smart with emotions.

Emotional intelligence is a skill that we all possess from birth. It is not a skill to acquire, but only to train. It's like a muscle. The more you prepare it, the more it will develop.

3. Why should I be interested in training emotional intelligence?

Emotional intelligence affects all areas of our lives. From a scientific point of view, research has shown that the level of emotional intelligence has a 55% impact on performance and success, understood as the ability to make effective decisions, as well as the quality of relationships, quality of life, physical and emotional well-being.

This means that the higher your emotional intelligence, the better your ability to make decisions, the better your work and personal relationships will be, and you will feel better physically and emotionally and be more satisfied.

Knowing our brain better, knowing how it works, what information it needs, how we make decisions, motivating and perceiving reality is fundamental to increasing our awareness and helping us to live better!

We are so bombarded with stimuli and information that being able to make effective decisions is fundamental. Besides, the World Economic Forum has included emotional intelligence among the ten skills to be developed for the world of work by 2020.

Jack Ma, founder of the Alibaba group, in his speech at the WEF meeting in Davos he stressed the importance of emotional intelligence also in the entrepreneurial and managerial field. We increasingly speak of artificial intelligence, of how robots will replace people in some jobs. However, there is a trait that will make us different from robots: our emotions.

4. How can we measure and train emotional intelligence?

Six Seconds, the largest network in the world of studies, research and development of emotional intelligence to which I also belong, has created, based on research, a self-assessment tool called SEI (Six Seconds Emotional Intelligence). This is scientifically based and validated and aims to investigate three areas, associated with eight emotional skills:

Know yourself

- Understanding emotions, giving them a name

- Recognizing emotional paths, what is your frequent pattern of action and reaction

Manage yourself

- Sequential thought: identifying the causes and consequences of what you do - Navigating emotions, it is not a matter of controlling or suffocating them, but knowing how to navigate them - intrinsic motivation: What drives you to do what you do? Are the factors of external or internal motivation?
- Optimism: how do you interpret reality? Can you see the opportunities?

Guide yourself

- Make empathy grow: Recognize emotions in other people and be able to connect with others -
- Pursue worthy goals: Align your daily choices with your sense of purpose and mission.

Through the SEI tool, you can have detail on what your starting level is in each of these areas and skills, what are your strengths and areas for improvement and then create a practical action plan to develop them.

5. I'm afraid of taking a low score on the test.

The SEI is a self-assessment tool. It is, therefore, about your perception. It is a photograph of your level of emotional intelligence at a given moment, not a sentence that says, "you have a low level, and you can't do anything about it."

The score itself means nothing. It is to have a measure of your starting point. It is not static and defined, but through training, it can be raised. If you repeat the test, after six months, you could get a different result!

6. What is the use of this test?

The SEI provides useful data to structure professional development paths, to improve one's leadership and, to improve one's life.

Become aware of the fact that, for example, we tend to control some emotions or let ourselves be overwhelmed by emotions, everything changes because it enables us to take concrete actions to improve this capacity.

7. And what benefits did you get from this tool?

I did this test during my certification path as an Assessor in emotional intelligence. I discovered that one of my areas of improvement was to navigate emotions. I found myself there. I had never had a good relationship with anger, and I almost felt like I didn't feel it. I tended to choke her. I decided to train this ability, taking note in a notebook of all the times I feel anger, and then I found "ecological" ways to download it, for example punching a pillow. It was liberating!

SIGNS OF LOW EMOTIONAL INTELLIGENCE

Low emotional intelligence is a problem that can affect all types of social relationships. Some experts even say that sensitive information can be more important than IQ to determine success. Remember that a victory that pays off makes you truly happy; that's what you achieve in your relationships with others.

That's why people with low emotional intelligence have so many difficulties to succeed. It is precisely their relationships with others that are problematic and lack several necessary ingredients to help them make good progress.

The term "emotional intelligence" is not well defined (some psychologists even say that there is no such thing). The reason is that EQ cannot be measured. Only for the "processing speed" of the brain, the processing power, measurable value is defined: IQ.

Of course, there are psychological characteristics of humans. There are various models, and a standard model is the Big 5, also the OCEAN model, which misses five factors: Openness, Conscientiousness, Extraversion, Agreeableness, Neuroticism. These factors are no better or worse. They are properties that are beneficial in some situations and harmful in others.

Example: Compatibility (Agreeableness). Assertiveness and the ability to defend one's point of view is positive in some (leadership) situations, as well as emotionally healthy. Elsewhere, empathy and consideration are required.

However, the ranking of a person on the "imperative scale" can hardly be changed arbitrarily, so the notion of "anyone can do anything" (which could perhaps be equated with high EQ) is misleading.

Also, there is no neutral assessment of when which behavior is right. Who judges objectively what the "right" response was? Again a human or a group. How should one then introduce a measured value? This is entirely different from the IQ because the time can be measured to work on, e.g., brainteasers.

CHARACTERISTIC OF PEOPLE WITH LOW EMOTIONAL INTELLIGENCE

Stress quickly

People with low emotional intelligence tend to stress because they do not healthily manage their emotions and get overwhelmed by what they are feeling. When we overload our feelings, they quickly become uncomfortable feelings of tension, stress, and anxiety.

People with poor emotional intelligence do not show their feelings and keep them trapped within themselves as a result as some negative emotions build up and create a mixture of anxiety, tension and stress. This is dangerous because these pent up emotions can lead to different health issues.

People with high emotional intelligence can manage their feelings by facing difficult situations on time. But those who lack this ability can find other ways to manage their emotions. Unfortunately, these means are not as effective as finding the solution before the problem gets worse. What is worse are the ways people with low emotional intelligence use to get rid of stress are usually destructive.

Difficulty in being assertive

Low assertiveness can lead to passive-aggressive behaviors. People with high EQ tend to strike a balance between good manners, empathy, and kindness, with the ability to remain assertive and set boundaries at the same time.

Limited Emotional Vocabulary

We all feel / experience emotions, but few people can accurately identify emotions as they arise / as we perceive them.

Unlabeled emotions -> generate misunderstandings -> lead to wrong choices and unproductive actions.

.

Concludes very quickly and tends to be defensive

People with low EQ tend to form opinions very quickly and get carried away by biased confirmations; that is, they only record the evidence that supports their view and ignores all the evidence that supports it. Contrary.

Grudge Guard

Unpleasant emotions serve a purpose. We should feel them, but we should not keep them and ruminate on them, generating resentment against others.

Don't

Move Away From Your Mistakes, Focusing on our mistakes makes us anxious and insecure. People with high EQ distance themselves healthily from their mistakes but do not forget them. This safe distance allows these errors to be "at hand" to be adjusted to become successes.

Feeling misunderstood

People with high EQ also often feel misunderstood because they do not always convey their ideas correctly, but try to adapt their speech until they are understood. People with low EQ (emotional quotient) often find it challenging to figure out how to clearly express this and it can lead to the unpleasant feeling of being misunderstood. Those with high emotional intelligence can have this problem too, but they know how and when to change thier approach to explain thier idea more explicitly.

Don't Know Your Emotional Triggers

We all have things that make us jump the lid. All. Knowing what these things are helps us not to be overwhelmed by them. Individuals with high EQ (emotional quotient) are usually aware of their triggers, and these triggers are things that can trigger particular emotions and make people act in a hurry. When you know which words and actions can trigger some adverse reaction, it helps you to avoid it. Try to avoid some situations, but people with low Emotional intelligence cannot predict your response to specific circumstances so they cannot prevent unpleasant consequences. You have already noticed these or other signs of low emotional intelligence in the people around you if so.

Never get angry

There is a misconception that people with high emotional intelligence are not mad. Being emotionally intelligent is not about being the right person, but about managing our emotions for the best possible results. Masking emotions are neither genuine nor productive. Always trying to show that we are not angry is not a healthy way to work with emotions.

Blame others for the way they make you feel

People with high emotional intelligence take responsibility for their emotions. No one can make us feel anything without our permission. They can influence and lead us there, of course, but ultimately, that reaction starts from our "permission." Although emotions arise automatically and unconsciously, we now have the option of choosing what to do with them.

Easily offended

People with high EQs are self-confident and can laugh at themselves. They can use humor in various situations, reframing many events that occur to them daily, without being offended. Of course, in conditions of exact offense and demotion, they make individual decisions in an attempt to resolve the situation.

Being unable to specify and name emotions

People with low EQ (emotional quotient) do not have an extensive emotional vocabulary. So even when they have experienced some excitement, they are unable to identify what they feel. To be fair only 36% of all people can do this properly anyway. If you do not know how you think because you cannot find a name for this emotion, it will not create a case for that right.

Unlabeled emotions tend to be misunderstood, and as a result, people make imprudent choices, while one person says he feels terrible another can differentiate between feeling anxious, worried, frustrated, sad or bored. The more you understand the word, the easier it is to understand what is needed, and that you are feeling this particular emotion and dealing with it.

Decrease the Importance of Emotions

People with low EQ (emotional quotient) may know that they are somehow different from others, which is why they often try to trivialize and minimize the role of emotions in our lives. A typical statement that you can hear from someone with low QE (quotient emotional) is that the only essential things in life are a sharp mind and logical thinking. At the same time you must remember that emotions help build functional relationships with others and communicate their ideas and opinions but that's not all, it also surprisingly involves emotional intelligence.

It is crucial for productive thinking, especially in a critical or risky situation.

CHAPTER 8
EMOTIONAL INTELLIGENCE IN THE ELDERLY

Recent studies tell us that emotional intelligence in the elderly is quite high on average. They value social relationships and take care of them. They know how to appreciate the present and regulate their emotions to adjust each moment. Besides, they evaluate their environment and what happens to them more positively. They see their reality calmer and more optimistic.

Some people may be astonished at the results of the work of the University of Texas and the University of California at Berkeley. Even today, we have a negative view of the elderly and the aging process. We associate time with physical decline, reduced cognitive abilities, and lack of permanent happiness, low motivation, and social and emotional isolation. In other words, we associate it with losses, especially to damages.

It is imperative to arrive in the fall to lead a healthy life. The less we have limits and the more we will know about the possibilities. It is also evident that the personality and circumstances of each plays a role in their consideration of life. The work we just talked about showed that the ability to manage one's emotions and to recognize one's feelings (as well as those of others) usually improves after age 60.

We are not talking about a normative thing. This does not mean that emotional intelligence for all is improved over time. The experience allows many people to manage the psychological processes well. He also emphasizes the priority given to one essential thing: social relations.

Emotional intelligence in the elderly

Getting older doesn't necessarily begin at 60, as that is when loneliness, dissatisfaction, and decline. You can at least go on for more than ten years. Life expectancy already exceeds 80 years. One could say that the age of 60 would be like a second adolescent. The 70 years are, in turn, a quiet maturity. Today we can all see something obvious: the elders are generally incredibly active.

They participate in endless dynamics in their communities, travel, and use their friends. They take care of their grandchildren and represent this constant and almost indispensable support for their children. Therefore, and even if many of these people need to see themselves often as a disease or emptiness of a loss against, a good majority of them have practical, emotional skills.

Theories explaining the rise of emotional intelligence in the elderly

Let's look at some hypotheses that, once collected, could explain the feeling of fullness that emanates from many older people:

- The theory of socio-emotional selectivity defines emotional intelligence. There comes a time when we realize that the quota of life is running out. This idea, this personal and existential reality, forces us to focus our attention on emotionally rewarding experiences. We do not care about future rewards. We want to feel good here and now because long-term plans become less critical.
- The theory of dynamic integration gives us another idea. Aging makes us gradually understand how much our physical and cognitive abilities are reduced. We are not as agile as before. We live by being conditioned by this pain in the hips, our diabetes, and

osteoarthritis. Faced with these uncontrollable realities, the older person chooses positive emotions. In this way, we can achieve balance and happiness. In the end, we can control our emotions.

- The emotional intelligence of the elders is also orchestrated through their experiences. Years have taught them to control certain emotional situations better. They understand their process, regulate themselves better, and know-how to connect to the needs of others.

- Another exciting and revealing factor is the famous "positivity effect." Some people, after taking stock of their life or their experiences, decide to keep only pleasant things. This point of view, this personal filter pushes them to see the positive side of things. You can create quality links and value everything with a more optimistic perspective.

Promote an emotional and intelligent maturity

Good emotional intelligence in older people means a better quality of life. Also, health indicators are linked to this factor. Proper management of our emotional world reduces stress or depression. It also improves all the everyday challenges facing adults: loss, illness, addiction.

Remember that emotional intelligence is not a normative thing. It does not appear with the years. We do not know what it is. And when we know it, we do not always apply the best strategies. Therefore, a new approach would be to use an emotional intelligence program for healthy seniors without a cognitive decline in each community.

It would be a matter of giving shape to multidisciplinary programs that would help anyone from their reality. Personal crises sometimes accompany older age. Wear, lack of motivation, and disillusionment are often present. The development of dimensions such as empathy, emotional regulation, or social skills, would significantly improve the aging process.

Consider the emotional intelligence of the elderly - and the elderly - as the key to good health, as the engine of a more vibrant, more integrated, and, of course, happier third age. We cannot forget that our life expectancy is increasing more and more. We, therefore, have the right to enjoy it intensively and to benefit from the best resources.

CHAPTER 9
EMOTIONAL INTELLIGENCE AND IMPACTS ON YOUR LIFE

They say that you cannot change what is not known, so if we want to change something in our lives, the first thing we should do is to know well what we intend to change. By the same rule, to avoid entering a depression, or to get out of it, the first thing we need to know is that a recession is the fatal outcome of the emotion of SADNESS when not only has it not been able to process, but that in addition, it has been feeding progressively and intensively. Therefore, let's get to know this emotion of sadness a little better.

From Emotional Intelligence, emotions are neither good nor bad, not even negative calls such as sadness, since they all fulfill a function for our survival. Emotions bring us an internal message, information about some need of ourselves so that we can take some action according to the information they transmit to us.

In this way, for emotions to be healthy and we can maintain an inner balance, they must be intense and brief, and precisely when we get caught in them and not managed properly, it is when they can become diseases (physical and mood). In the case at hand, when we get caught up in the emotion of SADNESS, and we don't know how to process it, it can end up choking us and resulting in a depression of greater or lesser intensity.

How to recognize and adequately manage sadness?

First, we must know that when we feel sad, it is because we have suffered some loss about something or someone important to us, or also when we do not get something we wanted. Then we feel discouraged, without strength or desire to do anything, and as the case may be, we quietly confine ourselves, crestfallen, we cry, and sometimes we even want to disappear. This is the way our body has to communicate that we should rest, recover, and reflect, then act.

If instead of doing this, we remain blocked in this discouragement, continually regretting our loss (or the grief for what we cannot achieve), and also feed it with limiting and destructive thoughts about ourselves and our abilities, then we will leave getting into an increasingly large hole, and we will lose all reaction capacity. The result, a depression!

Therefore, the way to manage this loss that we have suffered and that produces the emotion of sadness consists of two phases: one of acceptance and another of pro-action (or preparation for action).

The acceptance phase is the grieving phase that, depending on the case and the person, has its cycle. For example, it is not the same to lose a loved one, as it is to lose a phone we like, however useful it may be for us. Both situations are losses, but they are not comparable in any way and, therefore, the duel we experience, that is, the phase of acceptance of the loss of each of them, will have a different duration.

Once, recognized, experienced and identified as "our" sadness, the duel ends when we end up accepting that loss, that is, when we go from asking "why me?" To asking, "how can I get out of this or how can I solve that?". And from there, it is when the second phase begins, that of pro-action, and that is when we stop feeling like passive victims and start to take a responsible role in the situation. It is when we take power over our lives and undertake a reflection and search for solutions. It is also when we begin to mobilize our energy and take action to transform our reality effectively.

To recognize and manage the emotion of SADNESS, we need to:

- Ask yourselves these questions: "What have I lost or I don't get?", "What reality do I need to accept?"
- Rest, recover, accept, remember other stressful situations that we have left before, also remember the internal resources that we have used on those occasions and that we have available, and finally, reflect to generate effective solutions.

Of course, it is not always possible to do this for yourself and without help, so it is essential to have the support of people around us. And if the situation is more worrisome, then turn to professionals who facilitate and guide us in this process of self-knowledge and emotion management.

The most important thing of all and the idea that I want to convey is that with the use of some emotional skills and, especially with adequate aptitude, the emotion of SADNESS can be managed so that it does not lead to depression or, in his case, to get out of it.

Something that can help us in this process is knowing that, although we cannot have control over our external reality and the events that occur in our lives, at least, we must understand that with the help of Emotional Intelligence and other disciplines (Coaching, NLP, EFT, etc.), we can have control over our internal reality, over what we think and how we react to what happens to us.

Thus, with the sum of a proactive attitude and an adequate emotional approach, it is possible to overcome the onslaught of life, to flow with it, maintaining our inner balance and sustainable well-being.

HOW EMOTIONAL INTELLIGENCE ENRICHES YOUR WORK

Are you a friendly, sensitive, empathic person? Can you understand how the other person feels? If so, know that you have the essential qualities to achieve professional success!

The broader term for such abilities is emotional intelligence (EQ). It complements all well-known Cognitive Intelligence (IQ). An in-depth analysis of competences conducted by Daniel Goleman showed that it is the first one that determines our professional success to the greatest extent.

Contrary to appearances, it is such features as empathy, the feeling of unity with other people, and above all the ability to recognize and deal with their own beliefs that are more desirable at work than the IQ. It is enough to present it in the example of group work. People who have a high level of emotional intelligence will work more effectively because they are open to others and can recognize and solve their own problems as well as the groups. As a result, the group avoids unnecessary quarrels and ineffective discussions, and comes to a consensus in a peaceful and controlled manner.

The primary determinant of emotional intelligence is self-awareness (the ability to recognize one's feelings, emotions), self-esteem (self-esteem), and self-control (controlled response to external stimuli and emotional states). Unlike the intelligence quotient, EQ is not dependent on inheritance or development in the early stages of childhood. Throughout our lives, we can shape, develop, and improve it.

If you are still skeptical about this issue, that emotional intelligence is the essential thing in professional success. Remember the most stressful or dangerous situation you have been in. Did you then think over the learned rules, or the first reaction of the organism were emotions visible through, for example, sweaty palms, and abdominal pain or frozen in a place caused by a shock?

It is emotions that allow us first to assess the situation and adapt our body to the right response. We stand still, to be able to focus on the assessment of the danger, and sweating hands is the adaptation of the body to better capture objects. As you can see, emotions take precedence in unusual situations. Fortunately, we can practice our emotional intelligence and control our emotions.

Why is emotional intelligence our strength?

First of all, you cannot understand the functioning of the whole world, without understanding yourself. This is the first step to be able to look critically at the people around us. Social competences, such as empathy, assertiveness, cooperation, are essential aspects of your personal life. It depends on it whether we will be the soul of the party, liked, and accepted. We will not achieve this only due to high IQ or scientific knowledge.

It is also worth realizing that during the interview, it is our qualities such as the ability to behave appropriately, the ease of establishing interpersonal relationships, understanding the situation, the skill of persuasion make up the first impression and can determine whether the employer will see us as a future employee.

HOW TO DEVELOP EMOTIONAL INTELLIGENCE AT WORK

Improve your self-awareness

The first step in developing emotional intelligence at work is self-awareness.

Therefore, you must observe your emotions. Find it out:

- What makes you happy;
- What makes you afraid;

- Which things make you frustrated;
- What makes you motivated, etc.

Next, notice how your thoughts and feelings are constructed.

In this way, it becomes possible to stop repeating standard behaviors and to control better your reactions, your line of reasoning, and the degree to which life's bad weather affects you.

Also, know your limits and respect them - having respect for yourself is also critical for you to be able to develop intellectually and to be able to remain calm even in the most complex situations in the corporate world.

Increase your self-confidence

Doubting your abilities can make you a reactive, negative person who will act closed to news and limit your creative process.

With that in mind, start developing your self-confidence. If a job has been given to you, it means that you can do it. So, try to do the best you can and believe you will do it.

For this, support for learning how to develop emotional intelligence is coaching or starting a therapy process with a psychologist.

These professionals will be able to help you identify the causes of low esteem, for example, and will develop it to the point of eliminating the mental blocks that are already etched into your subconscious.

Learn how to deal with negative emotions.

Negative emotions are inevitable, and having emotional intelligence does not mean going into denial about those emotions.

However, it is essential to redefine these feelings, to be able to control the impulses and to understand the reasons why the situations in question are generating such feelings.

Therefore, seek to question yourself about the motivation of your emotions always. This way, in addition to having control, you will be able to find wiser solutions to your problems.

The corporate environment often makes us insecure, but it is necessary to be more rational and create acts based on analysis and consideration so as not to act wrongly.

Learn how to handle everyday pressure

One way to develop emotional intelligence at work is to be able to cope with the stress of everyday life.

Try to think calmly, even if the circumstances around you are agitated. Remember that something can only affect you if you allow it.

Seek to do your job the best you can, maintain your productivity, and analyze situations in a balanced way.

Getting in a hurry to get things done to escape the pressure of everyday life is pointless, so do it dynamically, but never in a hurry and without revisions. This way, you avoid mistakes and save time.

It is also interesting to create a schedule of your activities so as not to miss the deadlines in the delivery of your projects and to be able to do everything with quality.

Develop empathy

Empathy is critical to emotional intelligence. With this in mind, understand that there are days when your boss will be more nervous, that your coworker will be less receptive, and that the reactions of those around you will not always be guided by rational thinking.

That way, you can put yourself in people's shoes and not take your reactions personally.

- Use emotion to deal with conflict;
- Focus on problem resolution;
- Explain to your companions that you are there to contribute, not to generate criticism and frustration.

Often, just a moment of silence and a subtler approach will set things right.

CHAPTER 10
EMOTIONAL INTELLIGENCE IN YOUR FAMILY LIFE

How is your family life? Do you feel happy as a father or as a mother? On a scale of 0 to 10, how much do you feel fulfilled with your family life?

We often respond to certain situations and then regret it. Even knowing what would be ideal to do, we are seized by a force that takes away our choice, and by the time we realize it is too late. This force is named: EMOTION, and although it seems harmless or invisible, it is present at all times in our lives, building or destroying relationships, either with ourselves or with others around us.

We live in a time when stress, pressure, and competitiveness in the workplace, schools, colleges, and daily routines, such as at home, are rising. Knowing how to deal with emotions in the face of everyday adversity while avoiding losing control is a critical differentiator between successful people.

But why do people today talk so much about how to deal with emotions to succeed and have a good quality of life? You, like me, have probably heard that people with the highest intelligence quotient - the great IQ - are the most successful in life. What you may not know is that there is another kind of intelligence, emotional intelligence, which seems to be the secret behind many successful people.

But what is emotional intelligence? Emotional intelligence: Recognizing feelings or emotions in yourself and others, knowing how to manage them, using them to motivate yourself and applying them in various daily relationships.

The way parents deal with emotional issues directly interferes with their children's behavior, as children tend to repeat their parents' behavior and adopt the same patterns in their lives as adults (within the coaching process we call this repeating pattern). Therefore, the whole family needs to look at their emotions and always be evaluating and modifying conditioned behaviors.

Emotional Intelligence must be worked out early at home and later in schools, and parents are the first emotional preparers of their children, here are some tips for building a healthy and quality-of-life family:

First, make a connection between you (parents and children). This is a critical step in any successful relationship.

Second, think about what qualities, characteristics, and capabilities would you like your child to have? So who do you have to be for your child to be able to develop these characteristics, qualities, and capabilities?

Third, maintain a constant dialogue, an open dialogue, which contributes to your emotional and social development, as much of human learning occurs through interaction.

Your actions speak more than many words. And communication is paramount to understanding what children are thinking, how they are acting, and how they are developing this emotional intelligence.

TIPS FOR THE BETTER QUALITY OF LIFE WITH EMOTIONAL INTELLIGENCE

Have healthy habits

Including more habits healthy in your routine is an excellent start to achieving a better life. Paying attention to food, sleep, and exercise are essential habits for the metabolic and endocrine functioning of our body, as well as avoiding stress and tension. Also, eliminating practices that harm your health (such as smoking, drinking, and drinking too much coffee) also, as this is critical to a healthier life.

Keep your mind active

Research published in the New England Journal of Medicine found that Alzheimer's has a higher incidence among people with low levels of education. Thus, activities such as reading and studying, or even games that stimulate thinking, are exercises that work the mind and reduce the risk of disease.

Learn to enjoy contact with nature

Disconnecting from the electronic world and work is a great way to connect with yourself. Visit places that allow communication with quality and are conducive to emptying your mind for a few moments and relaxing. Focus more on your own emotions and feelings and contemplate.

Be optimist

Positive attitudes improve well-being and decrease the risk of illness by keeping the mind healthier. Try to invest in things that you enjoy and that do you good, and leave aside evil thoughts. Studies indicate that cultivating optimism reduces the risk of heart attack and stroke.

Accept yourself

Try to see the side positive of the things you have achieved. This is not to say that you should accommodate yourself when the situation is terrible: seek change within your means without despair.

Develop your Emotional Intelligence

By developing Emotional Intelligence, you can identify and control your emotions, and thus eliminate stress, frustration, and tension. If you want to have a better quality of life, get to know the Lotus Method, and see the many positive changes that will be increased in your life.

CHAPTER 11
BEHAVING LIKE A HIGH EMOTIONAL INTELLIGENCE PERSON

You think that if you don't cry, it will mean that you are emotionally healthy.

Quite the opposite. Crying is a symptom of being in tune with yourself and knowing that you are essential. You take care, and you love yourself, you respect yourself.

Crying is manifesting your emotions; it is transmitting what the energy of passion is asking you. To silence that energy is to generate a conflict that will fill your body with hormones to which you will not give way. Crying is not a sign of weakness; even men cry.

Do not pay attention to nonverbal cues.

Most of our communication is nonverbal. So being able to read between the lines (or between gestures) is essential for excellent conversation.

We must not forget how important it is to look at the other person in the eye when we speak, and it is a symptom of trust, transparency, and respect for the person in front of you. But beware! Beware of going through nonverbal cues:

- Make excessive movements with your arms or gesturing too much. It can transmit nervousness and lack of confidence. Use gestures only to emphasize your words.
- Shake hands firmly when you say hello. Eye contact is as important as physical contact. Be sure to give a good impression by transmitting strength and confidence in yourself when you shake hands.
- Keep a safe distance. Do not interfere in the living space of other people; being too close could be seen as an invasion of the privacy of the person in front of you and being too far away could mean a lack of trust and social skills.
- Crossed arms. Although this position often means stiffness, and it seems that you are showing a slightly flexible posture, it does not always mean that. Maybe the person in front of you feels comfortable or prefers to have their arms

crossed before letting your hands shake. You have to look at all the possibilities!

- Be careful with your body posture. The posture of your body gives a lot of information: if you are ungainly, leaning forward, "spilled" in the chair ... Any aspect can provide clues that the other person can interpret.

When people get angry around you, you think it was your fault.

Or do you think it was because of something you said or did? The world does not revolve around us or conspire against our person!

If you are focused on the negative that the people around you want to hurt you or that you are to blame for all the misfortune of the people around you. We are going wrong. Nor does it help that you want to be responsible for the accidents of others. Each one of us is responsible for his own life. Don't lose that weight.

If you have low emotional intelligence, you likely have low self-esteem, which makes you focus on the fact that everything negative that happens near you is your fault. And it's not like that at all! Having developed emotional intelligence helps us take charge of our lives, stop being victims, and be protagonists.

You always regret the things you said or did when you were angry.

Repentance is a clear sign of low emotional intelligence or poor emotional management. It's like permitting your negative emotions (although I don't like to call them that) to take control of your life.

Instead of feeling guilty about what you do, your job should be to evaluate the actions you did in the past and learn from them.

What made you lose your temper and get angry? What would you need to control next time? What altered you the most? The first step to remaining calm in times of high agitation is to know oneself: weaknesses, strengths, limitations.

It is said that "We own our thoughts and are slaves of our words." Then change your low emotional intelligence and cultivate self-control, emotional management, and temperance.

Find out what are the thought patterns that make you lose control and say what you don't want to say when you get angry. That is the only key to emotional management.

You tell yourself, "I can't change."

Your thoughts are fundamental, and if you block yourself the ability to grow, you can never move forward.

Your thoughts create your reality, and if you define yourself as a person unable to change, you are cutting off all your wings. Also, it is not true that it cannot be changed.

Don't "tag yourself." Leave the words "impossible" out of your mind, as well as the words "I can't" ... because you can and because everything is possible if you believe.

Training your emotions will help you know what your weaknesses are and how to strengthen your strengths to leverage change.

When you increase your emotional intelligence, it increases your quality of life. Your confidence, your self-esteem, your ability to remake yourself after a problem are emotional skills that will help you live more fully and have more control over your thoughts and feelings.

CONCLUSION

Emotional intelligence is vital in people's lives, being balanced in an emotional reaction, knowing how to control emotions and feelings, knowing oneself, and motivating oneself.

This gives the person the ability to be a better person, with better relationships, and affects what he will do in his personal and professional life.

The goal is to achieve a mature personality, which is the existential and dynamic set of physical, temperamental, affective, and volitional characteristics, which make us unique and original.

Emotional Intelligence no longer depends on the heart. It depends on the superior intellectual abilities of man, since a primitive brain such as the limbic system must be subordinated to a more advanced mind, the more control we have of our mind, the faster our connections are between the primitive brain and the cerebral cortex and the more emotional intelligence we will have.

To achieve the connections, we will have to create positive habits about emotions, which will make our synapses work better and faster.

Developing emotional intelligence will make us better people and help us to help others.

The actions we create in our lives are mostly based on our emotions and emotional intelligence. It makes sense that when individuals have an excellent knowledge of communication and organizational skills, they will be led to have the ability to make the right decisions and interactions with others. What we learn from our own emotions will allow us to pursue the lifestyle we want to live and create more of what we want in our lives, rather than what we don't want.

Emotional intelligence is a trait that can always be nourished and strengthened in all of us, but without having a developed sense of this, individuals will lack loving friendships, inner happiness and will generally be relegated to living a life of low social functioning.

Emotional Intelligence is the combination of emotion, reason, and brain, and as demonstrated, we have come to the definition that Emotional Intelligence is a useful contribution to business management. A person who is okay with himself can do much more to a company than a guy who brings all his problems to the company, causing his production to fall, and thereby disrupting all others who work directly with him. Then, by working on this intelligence, the subject would channel his emotions to the appropriate times, and learn to deal with all his feelings and to be guided by reason.

To stimulate this concept, a project of help for the interaction between the physical and social environment must be outlined, that is, encouraging the subject from an early age, at school, at home, on the street, etc. Emotional Intelligence should be implemented in the labor market as it would bring many benefits and help increase productivity.

www.ingramcontent.com/pod-product-compliance
Lightning Source LLC
Chambersburg PA
CBHW050729030426
42336CB00012B/1483